LIVING WITH A PEACE OF MIND

Ehimwenma Aimiuwu

Edofolks.com
Kennesaw, Georgia. USA.

© 2006 by Ehimwenma E. Aimiuwu
All rights reserved.

No part of this book may be reproduced, stored, in a retrieval system, or transmitted by any means, electronic, mechanical, photocopying, recording, or otherwise, without written permission from the author.

Library of Congress Control Number: 2006909801

Edofolks.com ISBN-10: 0-9791244-0-9
Edofolks.com ISBN-13: 978-0-9791244-0-2

Published by:

Edofolks.com
Kennesaw, Georgia. USA.

Book Website: www.edofolks.com/living
Blog Articles: www.blogcharm.com/edofolks

Printed in the United States of America

Dedication

This book is dedicated to my friend who lost his life due to economic hardship and loss of self pride.

Since I came to Atlanta, Georgia in 2000, I have noticed that a lot of educated young men, especially of African descent, are depressed and discouraged by their economic and employment conditions. Many of them feel hopeless and disvalued because their education appears to be a wasted investment. Their expectations after graduation have not materialized, which leads to all kinds of emotional, physical, and social instabilities.

I also dedicate this book to everyone in a similar situation or anyone who has gone through such an experience. I thank God for keeping the rest of us alive, safe, and healthy. I also believe that this book will inspire us to be blessed.

Content

Understanding who you really are	1
Have courage to take the necessary steps	12
Determination to stay on your path	24
Confidence to appreciate the steps you have taken	39
Respect for others who are different	47
Be truthful towards yourself	55
Be tactful as you move towards your goal	67
You must add value to your life	75
Utilize every opportunity for accomplishment	92
About the Author	102

Acknowledgement

I will like to acknowledge God almighty for giving me the gift of discernment, knowledge, and understanding. I also will like to thank Him for being within and around me all through my life.

I also thank the readers for buying my book and/or giving it as a gift to others. I also would like to thank the Redeemed Christian Church of God – Victory International Center in Mableton, Georgia for giving me the opportunity to be a worker and to serve in the church. The church has being a blessing and an inspiration in my life.

God bless my family. Special thanks to my wife – Kehinde, my son – Ehimwenma II, and my precious baby girl – Esosa.

Foreword

The purpose of writing this book is to encourage others in situations similar to my own to never lose hope about their success and their future. It is not only because God is in charge, but also because life gives everyone a fair chance to make the best out of what they have. It is only up to us to be patient and let life take its course.

We are usually in a rush to make money or have more power and status, even if it means lying about ourselves or others to get it. The truth is that when we are in a hurry to get rich quick and do not care what we do to others, the success is only temporary. Life and the world favor those who are patient, play by the rules of life, and gradually and respectfully accomplish their goals. We tend not to see this because humans today are in so much of a hurry that many have become short minded and hot tempered individuals. We have trained ourselves to see and celebrate quick successes, but ignore the gigantic successes that are built quietly and slowly through generations and stand the test of time.

A lot of people sometimes get frustrated when life is not going the way they think it should or the way they have planned it. They get angry and begin to wonder if God really exists, what life is all about, and if it even pays to be good. The truth is that you will never find satisfaction until you learn to abide by the laws of nature. This is the only way that you can achieve a peace of mind. After all, the man with peace of mind is the wealthiest man.

Have you heard that the healthy man is a wealthy man? Have you not heard that the richest man with bad health is actually very poor? Wealth is not only how much money you make, but it is also how much you have saved. People that lack peace of mind do not really save much. They are never satisfied with themselves and always have to pay someone else so that they can keep up with others. They worry about acquiring material wealth, the physical qualities of their sexual partner, status, and power. People focused on such concerns are not spending enough time with their children, and are simply not in the right mental and physical state to compete politically and economically with the rest of society.

All these worries eventually lead to poverty, because even if the money and power comes, it is not worth much if you can't comfortably enjoy it. So the healthiest man is actually the wealthiest man, because a man with a sound mind usually is not sick and does not have much to worry about as long as he follows the rules of life patiently.

There are many rules in life that can be interpreted in more than a thousand ways, but I will focus on just nine that I believe transcend both the ancient and modern cultures, across various races of peoples, as well as time and religious differences.

These rules of life, along with patience, include: understanding who you really are, having courage to take necessary steps, determination to stay on your path, confidence to appreciate the steps you have taken, respect for others who are different, being truthful towards yourself, being tactful as you move towards your goals, adding value to your life, and utilizing every opportunity to accomplish something.

As we read on, let us see how we can live a fuller life by following each of the rules found in Biblical principles, ancient proverbs, folktales, and just pure common sense explanations. At the end of it all, I hope that by living patient and descent lives, we can utilize these principles towards accomplishing our life's desires and ultimately begin living with peace of mind.

Understanding Who You Really Are

The biggest problem in the world today is that many people do not know or understand who they really are. Their entire life is based on some culture or tradition that needs to be done away with. They belong to a certain position in their family and so, therefore, have specific, prescribed roles to play, or are confined by their place in society. Some even live a life that is not their own. They live the life their parents want them to live or that they, themselves, feel they should have lived. I know people who choose occupations based on family, not personal, desires. Some are even told what classes to take in college if they want the tuition paid by the family.

It has been said that the richest place in any community is the grave yard or the cemetery. This is because large portions of the world's population leave this world never having found their purpose on earth. They depart the earth doing a job they were never happy with, thereby not having living a fulfilled life. The ultimate goal of life is to be happy without regret. That should be the purpose of education, be it formal or informal. Degrees should not be given if students have not been equipped with the knowledge of who they really are and what will make them happy.

People get degrees today to make sure that when they get a job, they fall in a higher paying bracket than those that do not have degrees. However, many employers are saying that having experience is superior to having a degree. Companies would prefer to pay a high school graduate with relevant experience $35,000 annually than pay an MBA graduate without experience the same salary. A good education, obviously, should provide practical experience in the areas that suit a student's personality and interests, and not focus on collecting tuitions to give degrees.

A lot of people in our generation are not taught by parents, school, career counselors, or even our educational system, to understand who they are. They are also not taught the benefit of charitable communal contribution, which is to enjoy whatever they are doing legally, even if they do not see an immediate financial return. Often they are forced to belong to certain groups that are obviously against the interests or development of the individual. Just because doctors, nurses, lawyers, and information technologists make good money does not mean that anyone should be certified in these fields, even if they can pass the certification exams. This leads to a society or generation that is frustrated and is prone to become violent and suicidal, especially if they have nowhere to turn.

There was a man named Jacob who later was named Israel. God had already promised his grandfather Abraham that he would not only make him a father of many nations, but God also promised him the inheritance of land and a seed by which the world would be blessed. Now, Jacob had to work seven years to get the woman he wanted to marry, but after the seven years of labor, he was given another woman he neither loved or cared about. Now, a man who has understanding for who he is would have bore the loss and moved on and allowed the conscience of the one who failed to leave up to his promise eat him from within. Better yet, he can get the legal system to work on his behalf, but instead, he chose to work for another seven years to get his desired bride. Now, the woman given to him was called Leah, but the one he loved was called Rachel (Gen 28: 10-15).

Why did the girls' father have to do this? Could it be that by the era's societal standard, Leah was very unattractive and had to give her away through trickery? Or could it be that it was really their culture and tradition that the eldest child must marry before the younger one? Regardless, as the story goes, Jacob had to work for fourteen years before he could get Rachel along with her older sister Leah. Jacob eventually had twelve sons representing the twelve tribes of Israel, but it was Leah, not Rachel, that fulfilled the covenant that God made with his grandfather Abraham. It was Leah who gave birth to Levi, the ancestor of Moses, who led them to them to the Promised Land from bondage. He is also the ancestors of the priests. She also gave birth to Judah, who is not only the ancestor of Jesus, but also the ancestor of the Kings of Israel (Gen 29: 13-35).

It is true that not everyone is fortunate enough to know his or her future through dreams, visions, or prophesy, but in the journey of life, you must persevere and be observant. Sometimes, we want something so much that we keep trying again and again, even if it takes us half our lives. We should come to a point where we ask ourselves, "Am I going the right way?", and, "Am I meant to be heading where I am going?" Then you must ask yourself, "What do I really need it for?" "Is it something I will enjoy doing while serving my community, or is it something I will enjoy because others are envious of it?" Are you learning a skill because you are curious of it and want to provide services others might need, even for a low pay, or you are doing it to earn the praise of neighbors? Well, a society that encourages the former becomes prosperous, while the later will lead to poverty, or what economists call "third world". People worshippers and praise seekers never live a life of their own; they live a life for others. They do not live a life that glorifies God through the happiness of serving their communities through skill or knowledge; they live life in search of public praise, even if the cost is private sadness. My grandmother often said that a small mud hut built on solid forest ground for many generations is of more use to the society than a skyscraper built on quicksand.

Jacob was a man who lacked the understanding of himself and his role in relation to the promise God had for him and his family. He wasted fourteen years of his life for a woman that he did not really know. What must have been the difference, anyway, between the two women, apart from physical qualities? It is not that he was sleeping with her, living with her, or spending quality time with her, or in any way really getting to know her. This was not a case of love at all; it was the case of the age old lust, which is as old as prostitution itself, if not older. Lust leads nowhere but to deceit and confusion. Lust is for temporary and outward pleasure. There is no future in it. A lot of men fall, fail, and lose because of the old adversary that makes almost every man an adulterer of the mind. Just because she has all the right fat in the right places does not mean that she can help make and keep a home, manage your money, plan for the future, believe in your dreams, respect your existence, or even raise respectable and healthy children. So what was it that Jacob saw that turned him from a man who was fortunate enough to have an assured promise and destiny revealed to him, unlike most men, to become a slave for   fourteen years?

    Not only was Rachel a thief that brought other forms of hardship to Jacob, God did not materialize the blessings of Jacob or make him prosper until after Rachel died. It was after her

Living With A Peace of Mind

death that Jacob began to have peace of mind. Why do we want what we want? Is it to serve our fellow man or to get the worship of our fellow man? Leah was given to Jacob, even though it was by deceit, to accomplish the promise and live a fulfilled life, but he wanted Rachel, I believe for lustful reasons, because she did absolutely nothing for him. In fact, it was because of Rachel's son Joseph, despite being a great man in his own right, that the children of God became slaves in Egypt (Gen 31: 19-35, Gen 47: 1-12, Exodus 1: 1-14).

    A person who knows and understands his or her destiny does not settle for anything. He or she does not waste time in a place that is not meant for him or her. In fact, whatever is given to you should be used as a tool towards your destiny or be thrown away. You do not want to waste precious time and energy on things that are obviously not meant for your destiny. It is better to be called arrogant and choosy than to live a life of frustration. Always remember that a zero will forever be greater than a negative one. It is better not to have anything than to have something that hinders you. Many have said that a rolling stone gathers no moss, but it is better to keep rolling until you fall by the riverside then stay fixed in the desert. You already know who you are and what will make you happy, so go find it. Do whatever you can to be happy as long as you do not harm or hinder another, because you will eventually have to pay for it, and that is no success at all.

In the parable of the talents, a wealthy master gave each of his three servants talents according to their ability. Talents, can be interpreted in several ways, and can mean anything from gifts of money, language, skill, knowledge, or even the ability to empower people. The servant who was given five talents made five more, the servant who received two talents made two more, and the servant who was granted one talent brought back exactly what was given to him.

It is important to remember that in this story the talents were given according to ability. Ability in this sense is the individual that has found his destiny or not. The previous two had found their destinies but the last one had not. Just because the two had jobs working under their master did not mean that they were not involved in other economic activities they had passion for that served their fellowmen. Maybe, they were language and science tutors; they could have had a coffee shop; they could have bought and sold merchandise on the side, or even had short term investments (Matthew 25: 14-30).

The servant that had five, probably made fifteen and brought ten back to his master, while the servant with two might have made six and brought four back to his master. People, who have found and are building their dreams on the side, usually use every opportunity they have to invest in that dream, which will eventually replace the job they currently hold. The two did not only enhance their lives, but also the lives of the one who gave or borrowed them the talents. It was this ability that they had that made the master give them more than the main subject of the parable.

While two servants invested their talents and multiplied them through various products and services to their fellowman, the individual who was given one talent went and hid it in the ground. The others maybe used the talents they were given to teach the world to learn and appreciate their language and culture, but the one talent loser would probably not even teach his children his language, not to mention creating a product with his gift. The others may have sat at a business table to impose rules and regulations of trade based on their history and understanding, while he thought that he had no history. When the others were defining themselves and finding their destinies, he settled for his current situation- a servant. Not only did this servant not prosper, he also prevented his master's money from working for the master.

I am sure if he had tried to find his destiny and had genuinely invested in a trade that resulted in a loss, the master would have appreciated him more. This is because he would have not only made an attempt to increase his master's fortune, but he also would have tried to better himself. We must remember that it is better not to have than to have something that holds you back. It is better to lose money in an attempt to grow it than to leave it sitting in the bank, which is still far more preferable than the ground. This is because you not only learn how to be a better investor or know where your skills and abilities lie, but most importantly, you must understand that money saved in the bank eventually loses value through inflation over time.

Usually, people like this servant are not just lazy; they are also very wicked and selfish. Their job is usually to discredit others and discourage the next generation. What individual has lived on earth and can not say he or she has found a skill to serve his or her fellowman with for free that others will eventually pay him or her for? There are millions of people in the world with abundant skills and dreams but do not have the resources to pursue it or are thinking of taking a loan to fund it. Here was a servant that was given what he needed for free to set his life on the right path, but he gladly refused. Do you know why? It was not his master's money that would change his life or bring him his blessing. Is it the bank that he refused to go to and invest the money that would now give him a better life? I am surprised that he even remembered that he was given the money. I wonder how he even remembered the spot on the ground to find it. A person with a vision and dream must stay away from servants like these because they are evil forces that prevent others from finding their destinies. Unfortunately, they outnumber the people who are determined to be the few living with a peace of mind.

Have Courage to Take the Necessary Steps

Many have testified to hearing voices within them, telling them what they should have done and what they should not have. It could be instruction about a life choice, in terms of spouse or career, or a decision about an action at that particular instant. Unfortunately, only a handful of people have the courage to follow what that voice is saying to them. Usually, it is not that the voice talking to them is that of Lucifer, the Devil, or that some evil will befall them if they abide by its instruction. It is simply a case of an individual's fear of failure. Usually, this voice does not follow what is popular in the world, or what is expected based on your family background. It is a voice that carves out a positive and unique path for each individual to follow. Sadly, this voice is often ignored for fear of being unique and being left behind on the ladder of success.

The response to the quality of this voice is based on the kind of company you keep. This is the most important foundation that determines the quality of life you will live and will serve as the basis of your children's upbringing. This is a situation of what goes in is what comes out. For instance, perhaps there is a woman who comes from a community of single mothers and feels that men are no good. She keeps company with single women who are also tired of men. Whenever a man approaches her, she gets advices from these same women. I would not be surprised if a voice never tells her to get married, but there may be a few exceptions. One day a voice might come to her and say, "You are burdened here; leave everyone and everything else behind, go to a new place, find a husband and start a family. This place and these people are preventing you from living with a peace of mind."

If such a voice spoke, she might not have the courage to obey it because she will be leaving her comfort zone and the people who make her feel "great" about herself and her situation. She might never even bring it up for discussion because she knows that those around her will shoot it down.

There could also be an individual who loved the arts, but comes from a family of acknowledged scientists. In their society, maybe art is less respected than science. Maybe artists do not make enough money, do not get enough recognition and status, and are not considered as intelligent as the science majors. So he forces himself to be good in the sciences and even chooses Engineering as a major. As time goes on, he is not really happy with what he does, despite the fact that he makes a lot of money. He is still extremely frustrated. Then a voice comes to him, "Why are you even here? Have you forgotten how you love to draw and paint abstracts into reality? You better get on the right track. Even if there is no money now, it does not mean that people will not enjoy paying you for your services later."

His decision now depends on the company he keeps. If he is in a company of fellow engineers, based on what they talk about and their interests, he might find it difficult to bring up the issue. This is because he does not want to lose his status in the group and create any doubt about his scientific abilities. What if he goes into the arts and he faces a reduction in pay and influence? Perhaps he is too old to go back to school to start another career with a wife and two children. Is it worth listening to the unwanted voice and taking art classes on the side, or quietly stick to the job that is not in his heart?

We do not have to always do what is cool and popular, or what will win us praise if our spirit is not at peace with it. That voice is the spirit within you that leads you to your destiny. There are good spirits and bad ones, it all depend on what you feed into yourself and the company you keep. Whatever spirit you have, a good one always intervenes or is present from within. You must always listen to that voice within that dares to challenge every step you take and encourages you to re-evaluate where you are heading.

There was once a man called Abram, who was later named Abraham; he was the grandfather of Jacob. As a young man, he was not very prosperous and was not fulfilled with life. He was married but childless; I guess that was why his nephew was so close to him. Now, he heard a voice from within and God told him to leave his country, his father's house, his family, and everything else for a strange land. Abraham obeyed but took his nephew with him. When he got to this new land, he had problems with the local people and his nephew, Lot. Eventually, he separated himself from his nephew and moved on with his mission. It was after this separation that

God fulfilled his promises to Abraham. It was after he left a nephew he was not supposed to take on his personal mission that God blessed him with children, material wealth, health and old age, and made a covenant with him forever that promised him land and seed that still exist to this day (Gen 12: 1-5, Gen 13: 1-18).

    Here, Abraham had the courage to take the necessary steps towards his destiny. He listened and obeyed the voice of God from within. If you notice, it was not the voice that told him to kill, harm, or hinder his fellowman through race, religion or gender, but the voice told him to prosper at the expense of no one else. This is the way you recognize the voice of the good spirit of God that dwells in all of us. It does not matter what religion you belong to, even if you are an atheist, we all have this voice in us. The choice to listen and obey comes from the company you keep, what you read, what you watch on TV, and the kind of things you love to listen to and get involved in. Just like a modern foreigner or immigrant, he was faced with hostility. There were times they would have killed him and taken his wife; but he persevered. At the end of the day, it was in a strange land that God prospered him beyond expectation, despite the fact that he was far away from his comfort zone and family.

Living With A Peace of Mind

There was also a man named John. He was the last great prophet before the new era of Christ. He was a lucky man because, unlike many men, he knew his destiny; all he had to do was follow the path that led to it. His mother was told that he was to prepare the way for Christ, and to help establish the new and right way of doing things. He was the first to bring forth the concept of baptism through water that symbolized the burial and the resurrection of Christ.

While his peers were eating meat and drinking wine, he was eating locust and wild honey. This was even during the civilized Roman era, where people wore linen, leather shoes, lived in brick or mud houses, and even used scents and perfumes. Our beloved John was in the wilderness wearing camel skin! My goodness!!! Was he mad or what? The answer is no, because a man on a mission is always unique and stands out. He does not dress, act, think, or do what the rest of society does, but at the same time, does not break the law while he improves the lives of others (Luke 1 & Luke 3).

An individual must focus on his or her purpose and do what ever it takes to avoid or minimize distractions and obstacles. This is the only way to maintain, coordinate, and achieve success. His mission was spiritual, and he had to avoid things like alcohol, women, parties, the latest fashion, and hair-dos. These things are not necessarily bad or evil, but depending of you goal or path of success, they can easily become a hindrance. While he was preparing the way for Christ, he met a lot of challenges. The Pharisees and Sadducees opposed him and challenged his authority to do strange things like baptism through water; they also wanted to know who this Christ was that was coming after him to baptize with fire and the Holy Spirit. The Jewish leaders were seriously upset with John and his mission of change. It takes great courage to bring change. There is not a man or woman in human history that brought change, positive or otherwise, without courage to the point of dying for their mission. When you have a mission you are prepared to die for then you have seen your destiny. You have known you mission and purpose towards your fellowman. We must muster the courage to walk towards this goal against all odds. After this is accomplished, you have begun living with a peace of mind. How do we know this? It was because John was extremely successful and he lived at peace.

Despite the fact that Israel was under Roman occupation and Jewish leaders were opposed to

Living With A Peace of Mind

John and his new culture, he impacted the Jewish citizens. People from far and near came to be baptized by him. He was so successful that even Jewish leaders would come by the riverside where he was baptizing. Not only that, he even baptized Jesus, and we were never told that he needed anything from anyone. Christ even testified of his success that of all men born of women, there is non greater than John. This proclamation assumedly includes Christ himself, because as a man, he too was born of woman (Matthew 11: 1-19).

What impresses me most about the success of John was that as he prospered in his service to his fellowman, he sent messengers to Christ to make sure he was the one to come. His messengers did bring back reports confirming Jesus' authenticity. He not only knew that it was time to move on to a bigger challenge, but he gave up his followers (or customers in the business sense) to go assist and join Christ in his mission. He was sent to prepare the way, but now he was contributing to the way. He went above the call of duty for what he loved and enjoyed doing. He enjoyed freeing the minds of the people from social and economic bondage to a spiritual fulfillment that surpassed all human endeavors and understanding.

After he was arrested by the King and Jewish leaders, despite appearances, his success and mission were not finished. Just like he had prepared the way by the riverside, on the streets, and on the temple leaders, he had to prepare the way in the palace too. Every society has its religious, economic, and political institutions. He had dealt with the previous two through the Jewish leaders and the masses respectively, now he was forced to focus on the palace and politics. He was so successful in his purpose and destiny that the King listened to no one else but John. After a hard day's work, most people like to relax in the evening by watching their favorite TV shows or movies, listen to good music, or what ever hobbies they enjoy before going to bed. The King soon made John his evening relaxation. John had previously condemned the King for marrying his brother's wife (the King's sister-in-law) while he was still free, but now the King enjoyed his company even though John was supposed to be suppressed in bondage. This is why Herod's stolen wife had him killed – because if John succeeded in converting the King, her tenure in the palace would be over (Mark 6: 17-29).

John did not die because he was a criminal or because he was in jail, he died because he was successful in his cause and had accomplished his purpose on earth. I pray that death meets us through our success and fulfillment in our service to mankind. I pray that we do not end up in the grave yard like those who did not have the understanding and courage to find and follow their destiny. Some people are born naturally, some have to go through surgery, and others through medication and pain killers. Some people die of old age, some of sickness, some are hanged or shot, and others have accidents or are lethally-injected. The truth is that it does not matter how you were born or how you die, the question is, "Did you find your destiny on how to serve your fellowman and did you have the courage to follow it through and be successful while enjoying it?"

While Jesus was on his way to Jerusalem, during his own mission to forgo his life for the forgiveness of sin and humanity's reconciliation with God; an external message came to him. It was the message of Lazarus' death. As soon as he received the message, the spirit and voice within him knew that part of the task was to go see his dead friend. He had a choice to keep moving on towards Jerusalem or to turn around and make a journey backwards. Now, keep in mind that if Jesus chose to go backward to accomplish a task in a town that he had already passed, he would be several days behind schedule. Is it proper to finish the race early or to finish the race properly by abiding by the rules of the game?

Jesus decided to go back, and he met strong opposition from his disciples for doing so. They claimed that the last time they were there they were not treated nicely and were rejected. The man with a purpose of living with a peace of mind reminded them that this journey, and the death of Lazarus, was part of his destiny to bring glory, not just to the one who sent him, but also to give assurance to those that followed him. To this day, the resurrection of Lazarus is one of the few things that sets Jesus apart from all other prophets and healers of his time. It was not a case of an individual dying or had just died on the bed at home, it was a case of someone that had died and had already been buried in a closed tomb for days (John 11).

Could it be that we miss out on our opportunity to find and fulfill our destiny because we refuse to obey the voice we are supposed to listen to, but normally refuse to do so due to age, time, peer pressure, money, or status? What person sees a light at the end of the tunnel and runs backwards unless he is hiding and does not want to be seen? There is no human that finds and understands his or her purpose, but still sits idle or confused. That purpose-driven individual will arise with all the motivation the earth can fathom and will drive to his or her destiny like a mad bull. This is the reason why we should never judge another, no matter how low we consider them, because the day the low finds his or her destiny, it is also the day he or she has risen above all that are yet to figure out what their purpose on earth is.

Determination to Stay on Your Path

Just because you have found and understand your purpose does not mean you are going to sail easily through and accomplish your goals without a strong will and sense of determination. A baby understands that to walk on two feet is human, but that does not mean he or she will accomplish it without first falling a couple of times and hitting his or her bottom on the floor. It is because you are unique that you have to be determined in every step you take to reach your destination. You must be aware that the dream killers are there and they enjoy seeing others end up just like themselves. It is called the spirit of unison and conformity. Many of them tend to be successful and the whole world hopes and wishes that they were like them, but you need to be careful, because they are not all living with a peace of mind. No one harms or hinders others and does not pay for it. It always appears that they get away with it, but if you are observant and patient, you will always see them gradually pay for their crimes. Unfortunately, it does not always stop with them, it moves to their next generation and on until they repent and give up what they harmed or hindered others for. Only those who have no vision or are just like them can never notice their decay.

How do I know all this? I am observant; I listen, and I watch. Have you not heard people say that "the evil that men do lives after them?" Is the world not continuous with each surviving living thing reproducing itself, despite the threat of extinction and disasters? What does each surviving living thing pass on to the next generation apart from blood and identity? I am sure they also pass on habits, culture, heritage, reputation, inheritance, and debts. Everything passed on could be good except for debt, because it is the first foundation of bondage. A man who has no debt is mightier that he who has everything including debts, because a man with no debt is highly at peace. He has the freedom to explore and excel without limitations to himself or society. Debt is everything and anything negative that you posses. It does not matter if you created it or you acquired it. Bad or sickened blood, financial woes, blood and slavery money, or even suspicious and unpleasant habits are all forms of debt. Debt is not only financial; it could be social, moral, and worst of all, spiritual. You will never be living with a peace of mind until you intentionally get rid of all your debts to the best of your ability. Did God not tell the husband of Queen Jezebel, King Ahab that he will visit his iniquities upon his descendants? Have you not heard of the God of Abraham, Isaac, and Jacob (1 Kings 21: 21, 1 Kings 21: 29, Exodus 3:6)?

Even if you do not believe in God, you will agree that creation, existence, evolution, or the "big bang" is all about continuation. So no matter how independent and individualistic you think you are, the life you live is not your own. Many debts started from your fathers and it will go to your children, even if you never met them. You must intentionally cancel all indebtedness to set your children's path towards the path of living with a peace of mind.

To eliminate all debts effectively, it must be done in the spirit because whatever manifests itself in the physical has already manifested itself in the spirit. Before the creation of the world, before the foundations of the universe, or before the "big bang" took place, God had already decided in the spiritual what would be manifested in the physical. According to the Bible, God agreed with the heavenly beings to make man in their own image (image of God Himself) before man became a physical being. In fact, God and Satan reached an agreement in the spiritual realm before calamity befell Job in the Physical realm (Gen 1: 26-27, Job 1: 6-12). What some people do not realize is that their success or failures are not necessarily their own doing, but how they react to it. Most of the time, our success and failures are based on the activities and visions of those that came before us as a family or society. I am sure that you have heard people say that we appear to see further than our ancestors because we stand on the shoulders of giants. We all have a great past and heritage because we all come from the creator of all things, but with time, mankind, out of greed and selfishness, has corrupted the systems. The best we can do is to correct and modify this system to better our lives and the lives of those coming after us.

Some of us have read or heard of the ancient world in the times of idolatry and magic, where some kings or head of homes made a spiritual commitment on behalf of themselves and their descendants to certain powers for wealth and protection. In fact, Abraham did this numerous times in the Bible to acknowledge the fact that he and his descendants will only and forever serve God (Gen 8:20-22, Gen 12:7, Gen 13:4, Gen 22). Usually, in the ancient kingdoms, like Rome and Egypt, and many secret societies, such contracts with spiritual powers require blood. These powers would demand human blood to show their seriousness and loyalty.

Was the crucifixion of Jesus a human sacrifice for God to replace the peace and burnt offerings of animals on altars? What about Abraham's acceptance of God's request to sacrifice Isaac? Often, people would also have to make a vow that their children or their first son must follow suite, or the covenant or agreement would be broken. What would have happened if Isaac or Jacob refused to follow God or if Abraham failed to teach them about God? Would God's covenant have been broken and nullified? When a certain priest did not raise his children in the ways of God and His covenant, his lineage was cut off (1 Samuel 3: 11-18).

Sometimes, an entire generation was forced to suffer for not following the covenant made by their ancestors (2 Kings 17:14-20, Jeremiah 11: 6-13). If this is so, what about those who made

Living With A Peace of Mind

spiritual commitment to demons and evil spirits as their god and used the blood of the captured? What happens to the covenant if broken by their descendants? It is usually the descendant, who comes many years later and has no idea of the deal that was made with their lives that suffers the most. If you are unaware of an ungodly covenant you are supposed to follow, how do you break it? You can not run away from these covenants. This is because they are covenants of blood (DNA) and spirit. Your DNA is your DNA and your spirit is your spirit. Some have tried to run away from their homes to another continent; some have married strangers just to dilute their race and to reduce discrimination on their children. Others have hidden their culture and identity with the hope that it will increase their chances in life. To their dismay, they are really no better off than the others they left behind or those that chose to remain true to themselves. They only transformed their problem from one form to another. There are families with the most educated, intelligent, and hardworking men, but they can never find the job they want, or every business they have tried has failed to yield a penny.

I will not speak of families with women so pretty that you would doubt the account of Helen's beauty in the Greek and Trojan wars, yet no man wants to marry. Even those that dare eventually either run away, die before the engagement, are imprisoned, or become deformed. This is not Voodoo; it is spirituality. We must be careful what we say and who we make agreements with. In Genesis 1, the entire creation took place by God's word – "And God said".

Instead of rising up with determination to reverse the direction of their lives, many people succumb to false pride and justification, without understanding the situation they find themselves in. Some of them are the ones who educate themselves and remind others that money is not only the root of all evil, but they should remember that it is very hard for a rich man to enter heaven. They will also be glad to inform you that money is not everything and it is not good to run after it. Well, it is not money that is evil; it is the love and worship of it. Yes, it is true that it is hard for a rich man to enter heaven, but it is even harder for the modern poor, because they are the ones directly responsible for most crimes. The big guys might fund the operation, but the impoverished are the ones who carry out the operations. They pull the trigger, they actually raid property, and they are the ones who take the blame when caught. If their poverty did not take them hostage, no crime would be committed. It is also true that money is

Living With A Peace of Mind

not everything, but you must provide a service that your fellowman must be willing to pay for to make a living.

Some have been known to use the goodness of freedom and liberty to promote their lonely agendas. Just because they come from a family or culture where men do not stay or come home at all, it has become justification as to why these men are either no-good or worthless. Instead of them to crying their souls up to God and using their prayerful lips to condemn any activity in the spiritual realm that wishes them loneliness, they begin to preach the gospel of single parenthood. Young girls are often told publicly that they do not need a man, a man will hold them back, and that a man will rape one in every three of them. They are also told that a man is only good for sex, and that they should be prepared and equipped to be a single mom. Just because some girls cannot find men or were raped, does not mean that all men fall into that category. It also does not give someone with a PhD the liberty and freedom to encourage young girls that have never been and will not ever be raped, who have loving fathers and uncles at home, to hate men and join them in their lonely crusades. Humans are social beings. If we do not have a family to love and verse visa, we will create social clubs, and in some cases, create gangs to belong to.

    Our culture has become a place where the men are so angry that they make violence a symbol of manhood. We now live in a culture where it is cool to sleep with as many women as possible, with the intention of getting them pregnant and taking no responsibility of it. It has become a way of life where men publicly say they are more prepared to go to jail than take care of their children, because it is the woman's job. We are now a society where parental age no longer matters and have young teen children reproducing themselves. It has become acceptable in our culture for fathers to be in jail and never get to know their children. This is the very culture of post-slavery that had crippled African-Americans today. African-American slavery, to me, was not just about politics, heritage, or economics; it was about total control of a free labor force. The success of this institution was achieved not just by turning families and clans against one another; it was achieved by eliminating the power, authority, and influence of the Black male. This is the debt African-Americans have yet to pay or cancel, either in the physical or the spiritual realm.

There are certain things that do not happen when a man is present. A father does no have to be extremely economically successful or a college graduate to be a good role model to his children. When a responsible father is present and has a voice, there is orderliness in that home, and when this occurrence is widespread, the entire community is benefited. I believe increased fatherhood in our communities can bring about effective change. These changes could be reducing high crime rates, teenage pregnancies, and high school drop-outs. It can also reduce the number of young Black men in jail, and increase Black marriages and property ownership.
You must be determined to get what you want. If you want it badly enough, you will do everything possible to get it, even if it becomes necessary to go to the spiritual realm. In the spiritual realm, you elevate yourself at no expense to anyone else.

When Jesus was about to start his mission of reconciling humanity to God, after he was given a baptism of graduation by John, the Devil came in the spirit to hinder and deviate him from his cause. The devil told him that if he was truly the son of God, he should turn stones to bread and eat. He knew that Jesus was not only living in the desert, but he had being fasting for forty days. The spirit did not just drive Jesus there to fast for the beginning of his mission, but also to fast against all forms of temptation and hindrance along the way. So, Jesus was not only prepared, but was determined to withstand this hinderer. This is why Jesus replied the devil by informing him that it was written that the word of God surpasses the power of hunger.

Many of you are aware that the strongest weapon in economic and political world is hunger. It is more effective than the fear of nuclear bombs. Nuclear bombs guarantee death, but hunger is the anticipation of death. Many consider the anticipation of death worse than death itself. With hunger, you can control a peoples' government, the power of their currency, their import and exports, or even how they marry and the number of children they should have (Matthew 4: 1-17). The devil was counting on the power of hunger in the desert as an advantage, but when he failed there, he took Jesus to the heights of the temple in the holy city and told him that if he was truly the son of God then he should jump down. The Devil went as far as quoting the word of God from the prophets, saying that it was written that the angles would come and attend to him and no harm could befall him.

Can you believe this? This biblical incident illustrates the importance of constant spiritual vigilance. If you do not fall outside in a strange land, you might fall at home in your comfort zone. So your guard might be up in public eyes, but it is in your home that you get drunk, use drugs, fight with your spouse, ignore your children, and yet still wear a mask of spirituality to cover all your bad habits. You might be able to fool your neighbor, but you cannot fool God.

The Devil took Jesus to his city and temple, and placed Christ high above it. He basically told Jesus that he was at home and should feel free to do whatever he wanted, as everyone would undoubtedly obey his instructions. Jesus replied that it was written that we should not put God to the test. Jesus was basically addressing the ugly side of freedom that destroys without moral principals. He was saying that just because he could, or had the right, or the freedom to think, say, or doing something, does not give him the weakness to go astray from his purpose. His goal was never to show he had power, but to withstand the Devil while he reconciled humanity to God.

Satan, still undaunted, then took Jesus to a high point and showed him the riches of the world. The very things that humans loved to fight, betray,

Living With A Peace of Mind 36

and kill each other for. The Devil had tried him with the emptiness and lack of the desert, the power of hunger that humanity hates, the complacency of his home, the sly disguise of freedom, and now wanted to hinder Christ through what humanity loves and cherishes. He told Jesus that he will give him the riches, power, and splendor of the world, only if he would bow down and worship him.

It should be obvious to everyone that, despite being evil, the Devil must be very stupid. If he could quote the word of God, how could he not understand that there was nothing created that was not created through Christ, including himself.

This situation would be like my son telling me that he would give me his mother for a wife if I worshiped him. Did I not marry his mother before I had him? The devil's proposal was ridiculous, and Jesus told him that it was written that we must worship God only. He then ordered the Devil to depart from him and the Devil was gone.

Although Jesus, as the son of God, didn't have much trouble with the Devil's last challenge, for most humans it is this last temptation that is the strongest. What can a person do to acquire wealth and power? Must you worship God through the

Living With A Peace of Mind

service of your fellowman, or should we kill, enslave, betray, steal, and lie to gain power and wealth, thus, becoming a servant of the Devil? The story of temptation shows the determination every person must face throughout his or her life. We tend to enter the world empty and are under the guidance of our parents. Then we begin to hunger for independence, and then we are free to become adults and set our rules. Soon, we begin to want to acquire some finances, wealth and recognition. Many wise men have said that you sleep on your bed the way you make it. It is the foundations that you have set as a child that usually help to determine and shape you future, unless something is done radically to change your path. The forces of hindrance and deviations come to you in all forms as you grow, to discourage you and misguide you from finding your life's purpose. It could be traditions, culture, friends, family, peer pressure, government, laws of the land, or even religion. As you get older and become an adult, it is the worst period. That is the time that the power of hindrance comes full force, in an attempt to make sure you die without living with a peace of mind, and never knowing or finding your life's purpose. You spend your days trying to play catch up in all the wrong places, either by competing with the others or trying to fit into some societal expectations. It has been said that you do

Living With A Peace of Mind

not praise or condemn a person until after his or her death. We must all ask, if he or she served his or her fellowman. Remember, that he who must be the greatest must first be the least. It is the service you provide with your talent and skills that you enjoy freely, which people are prepared to spend their time and money on that helps to define your quality of life.

Confidence to Appreciate the Steps You Have Taken

A lot of us, who are very used to our comfortable environments, find it very hard to take one step without first looking back, and then wondering if it was worth taking the step at all. Many are scared of what others would, or might say, about them acting differently, or are scared to try and accomplish what nobody in their blood line has done or attempted before. Many like to conform, so that no one will tell them later the famous line, "I told you so." After you have taken that first step, and a couple others, have the courage and determination to continue towards your dream. There is nothing wrong in looking back just to make sure that nothing is left undone, or if you have walked a bit out of line, as long as you know that it is just a cross-check in an attempt to press forward again. Many who walk today once fell a thousand times with tears in their eyes, until they acquired the confidence to take a couple of steps without falling.

There was once a young prophet in the Old Testament, who was sent by God on a certain mission. He was clearly instructed by God not to eat anything on his mission until he got home from the region he sent him to. He did go on the mission and successfully did what God told him to do, but on his way home, he met an old respectable prophet. The old prophet told him that God had asked him to invite the young prophet into his house. When they got to the old prophet's house, they ate, and the young prophet left for home. On his way home, he was killed and eaten by a lion.

When I first read this story, I was mad at God and His lousy old prophet for leading the young and promising prophet astray. I began to ask myself why an old experienced prophet would lie and deceive a younger prophet. I wondered why God did not give the young prophet a second chance to learn from his mistake. Does the body of God work against itself? Why didn't God send the fire of Sodom and Gomorrah on this old wicked prophet? I was terribly upset by the whole incident because I could not understand why out of all the people in the world, it was God's prophet that would hinder another prophet of God and not the Devil (1 Kings 13).

As I was exercising my free will to be angry, a voice spoke to me saying, "my mission is my mission and for no one else. If God gave a command or a mission, follow it through unless God changes it Himself. The God that revealed an instruction to you can also reveal another direction to you in the process." I began to wonder why God did not use the old prophet to begin with; after all, he was in the region. Why would God use a younger prophet with no experience from a distance? Could it be that this old prophet had fallen out of favor with God? Was it out of jealousy and envy that the old prophet tricked his younger colleague to death? Or could it be that God and the old prophet planned to kill him for some reason? Many might say that God sent the old prophet to test the young one. If this was so, should the young prophet have disobeyed a new instruction from God if he truly felt that it was God who sent the old prophet to him? I believe the old Prophet had fallen out of favor with God, and knowing how God usually operated in such mission, he now chose to become an agent of the hinderer after he heard that the young prophet was in town doing God's work.

The ultimate question is, "why did the young prophet fail?" Did he think he had completed God's work, so it did not matter now if he ate? Did he think he was out of the region of the assignment and so was safe? Or did he have too much respect for the old prophet and thought he was above telling lies? You see, a lot of people in my generation are people worshippers and lose their concentration too quickly when they meet people they look up to. Even when they know they are right and have the necessary information to do things correctly, they would always allow one general, a chief, an elder, or some authoritative figure to mess things up like it is done in many third world nations. A lot of people lose out in the culture of confidence and allow themselves to be robbed of their dreams by a few who have status and power.

In many third world countries, it is the custom that the elder is always right even if he is drunk and does not have a clue about the subject matter. It does not matter the quality of education, experience, or technological advancement a younger person acquires in more advanced nations. When he gets back to his country, he is still placed under the authority of some elder, who might have been in the government for over forty years and has not a single accomplishment to his name.

Many third world countries have developed a culture of title and respect, without responsibility. Foreigners wonder why there are some many churches and universities in many third world nations, but no significant sign of progress in politics, economics, and social infrastructure. This is because, like the young prophet, the Christians or the youths have not developed their culture of confidence in accomplishing their dream over the traditional standard of respect without responsibility. The prophet failed to stand up to the older and obviously more experienced colleague, despite the fact that he knew he must have been out of favor with God. In order not to offend him, or he believed blindly that he was speaking the truth, gave up on his dream by submitting himself to a tradition that led to his death.

A person who has found his or her mission, who has found the determination and courage to follow through, must also have the confidence to push through all traditional, cultural, and social obstacles even if it leads to ridicule, shames, and rejection. People who get angry because you did not listen to them on your way to your success are people who have nothing better to do. They are also people who have either missed their calling or would like to share in the glory of your mission for

Living With A Peace of Mind 44

free. It does not matter which way they come, they are all hindrances that need to be put aside. Many of these title holders without responsibility are those that have lost their bearing and are only trying to save face by acting like they are giving you the advice necessary to do well in life. They are all parasites. If they can not make their own way, they want to share in yours by using their titles over you. The failure of the young prophet to be confident in his mission against the old prophet's title is what killed him. A lot of young people in many places have become discouraged and visionless because of issues like this, and they genuinely need to pray for the spirit of confidence against all odds.

In the story of Jesus and the Canaanite woman, it was obvious that Jesus, as a Jewish man, culturally and legally looked down on the Gentiles. His mission was to bring salvation to the house of Israel while he was alive and his disciples were to take the salvation to the Gentiles after his departure. On this occasion, a Gentile woman needed a miracle from Jesus, but Jesus was not willing to give it because at the time, he was focusing on the Jews. Jesus did not want to give the food that was meant for the children (Jews) to the dogs (Gentiles), but the Gentile woman made it clear that even the dogs eat the food that fell off

Living With A Peace of Mind

the children's plates. What the Gentile woman was saying was that no matter what was meant for the Jews, some of it will trickle down to the Gentiles sooner or later. This was true and obvious, to the extent that Jesus could not deny it, and had but no choice to give her what she asked for (Matthew 15: 21-28, Acts 10: 27-28).

It was the woman's confidence in the nature of things, that persistence and knowledge will always conquer all. She understood that Jesus was the messiah; she understood that he could heal her son, and knew that God's blessing was for all of humanity either now or later. When you have the understanding of societal laws or the laws of natural forces, you become unstoppable. No one, no matter the race, status, gender, or power they believe they have, possess anything compared to what this law provides. This increases your confidence in what you do and how you do it. Knowledge in not only power, but it is also the foundation of confidence. It was this confidence that healed her son and nothing else. Jesus then replied by saying that he had never seen such faith in the whole of Israel. Jesus was indirectly saying that he has not seen such confidence among his own people in the matters of God. He was implying that this Gentile woman had more knowledge and understanding of the God of Israel

Living With A Peace of Mind

more than the Israelites. While the Israelites were wondering if Jesus was the messiah or not and asking themselves by what authority he was healing on a Sabbath day, the Gentile woman was already being blessed by his mission on earth.

If we must live with a peace of mind, we must make sure that we live up to expectations in whatever we do; but in whatever we do, we must make sure it is what we enjoy doing, no matter what. There is no one who enjoys doing what he does not know or understand. There is no one who does not spend time in what he or she enjoys. As long as you spend time on something you will become a master of the thing. When you then master what you enjoy and people are willing to compensate you for it as a good or service, you are already on your way to living with a peace of mind.

Respect for Other Who Are Different

In life, you must meet people who are nasty and who have little or no manners or courtesy. There will also be those who are racist and sexist, who are arrogant, who are negative, and who have a hobby of looking and talking down on people. These are people you must avoid at all cost; but ultimately, you must respect everyone no matter how different they are. Just because you respect their difference does not mean you must be best of friends, and it does not mean that they do not have anything to offer in some areas. It was once said that you meet your destiny on the road you chose to avoid. This means that what you really need to make you live with a peace of mind might be with the people or path you have rejected. The necessary information that will make a change in your life forever might not be with your friends or loved ones; it might be with some strangers who do not act properly or are different.

There was a time when Saul, Israel's first king, went into battle against a nation that did not serve the creator. He was ordered to destroy the people completely. While the war was going on, Saul needed some advice from his prophet, whose name was Samuel. Unfortunately, Samuel had recently died and God was no longer communicating with Saul like before. As he waited for the word of God that he needed to complete his task, he got desperate. Under the cover of the night, King Saul disguised himself and went to the witch of the culture they were trying to destroy for assistance. When Saul got there, he made his request known to the witch but the witch did not know who he was because of his disguise. The witch went ahead to perform her duties and funnily enough, the spirit of Prophet Samuel arose to deliver the message from God. It was then that the witch realized the identity of her customer. It was the King of the Israelites himself in disguise, and he has used her to get the information he needed (1 Samuel 28).

Just because the elevator is quicker and more effective in moving through tall buildings

Living With A Peace of Mind

does not mean that the staircase will not eventually get you there. It might take a longer time and be more stressful (not to mention physically challenging), but you will eventually get there. We usually realize it when all we have believed in or planned for fails. It is the day that the elevator breaks down that people remember that the building has stairs. The poster needed to inspire and change people's lives forever has always been posted on the stairway and not in the glamorous elevator. It is sometimes in a place or thing that we have rejected, and have defined as inferior, that the blessing of God that would change your life around might be found.

We must respect everything God has made. It does not matter how our culture, traditions, or religion defines it. We must respect it even if we do not accept it. There are people ignored because of their race, sexuality, gender, age, occupation, parental status, religion, culture, and economic status, but yet have so much to offer. They might not fit into the popular or acceptable norms of the community, but it does not mean that they do not have the information, means, or human connections that will give you the key to the missing links of your success story. Everyone has something to offer.

There was once a Syrian general who had leprosy and his Jewish servant told him to see one of the prophets for assistance. When the general met with the prophet, he was advised to swim seven times in the River Jordan and his illness would be cured. This made the general feel insulted because Syria was a higher civilization than Israel and was a reigning political power at the time. Why would he leave his land to go swim in the territory of his subjects and opponents? Do you tell an American senior government official to go buy his medicine in Iran, or better yet, to go and swim in Saddam Hussein's swimming pool for a cure? So you can imagine the courage it took to swallow his political and racial pride. He then went to swim in the river Jordan as advised, and he received his healing, as assured (2 Kings 5: 1-14).

Lack of respect and pride in some heritage or political supremacy can hinder you from living a fulfilled life. One of the best ways God humbles or humiliates people is to put their joy in a place they feel is beneath them. Until you learn to humble yourself and respect others totally unlike you, you might be lowering your expectations of living with a peace of mind. Do not die and be lying in the graveyard not knowing all you needed to know and appreciate. Do not leave this planet physically or spiritually without achieving your

100%, because a life half or partially fulfilled is still a waste. An individual willing to live a fulfilled life must be prepared to know or learn what is inferior or is hidden by cultural bias. Even if you choose not to follow it, know why.

Many individuals have gone to the beyond without fulfilling a tenth of their purpose here and, thereby, lived a somewhat dissatisfied life, even by their own standards. They refused to genuinely acknowledge, learn, or even experience a different culture, religion, ideology or a meaningful racial relationship that they were merely raised to disagree with. This might or would have been the foundation of arriving at or fulfilling an accomplished peaceful life. In an attempt to blame someone else and lift the burden off their shoulders, it was the teaching of their ancestors and heritage of their past that they so revered that became their stumbling block in fulfilling God's mission for their lives. You must choose one, because you can not serve both. You must either choose happiness with a peace of mind or choose frustration. You must either choose a life of eternal fulfillment or choose an existence limited by pride and ignorance.

Sometimes, it is those rejected individuals, who could be single-mothers, the economically disadvantaged, orphans, minorities, homosexuals, prostitutes, the unemployed, homeless people, or teenage parents, that eventually arrive at their fulfilled destinations. It is through perseverance, change of habits and beliefs, along with some courage and determination, which allow someone to overcome all odds against societal statistics. They rise up in their later years, despite intentional social opposition and positively impact their communities and nations like no other group. Some even end up changing the social definition that stereotypically placed them in their sub groups. While most are content with their misguided achievement, which is usually acquired through frustration and pain, they gradually move towards their destination in style, accomplishing for themselves what most people never understand how to do.

For example, when I was in grade school, many of the children of the rich politicians and businessmen would sit at the back of the class feeling big and cool. They would never take part in any extra-curricular activity because they felt it was beneath them. They enjoyed being rude to teachers and school prefects. At the same time, many of the middle and lower class children humbly sat in front of the class, were obedient, and did what ever they where asked to do. While the former felt they were worth a dime because of their parents' accomplishments, those less privileged children were discovering their talents for the future through extra-curricular activities. To this day, many of these students' economic foundations are based on the hard work, skills, and determination they have acquired (Luke 18: 9-14).

In another story, the "destiny of mankind" came to rejoice with those who had accomplished their mission on earth. So he had a banquet and invited the world to it. His aim was to see who was ready and who was not focused in achieving his or her mission. Only those who were prepared in whatever trade in life and had contributed a lot to their environment freely and peacefully would attend the banquet. So, he started out by inviting the richest and most notable people by the world's standard to the banquet, but they all failed to make the banquet because they were still in search of their various purposes. They gave all kinds of excuses as to why they were not ready to attend the banquet. The excuses ranged from family, economic, pleasure, social, and political issues. This made the host of the banquet very mad that he ordered his servant to go get all forms of rejected elements in society to come in for his banquet. Contrarily to expectation, they all came in and filled the banquet hall (Luke 14: 15-24).

Living With A Peace of Mind

Just because some individuals are at a lower economic and social-political status, and live short and socially restricted lives, does not mean that they do not achieve the state of living with a peace of mind by the end of their lives. Just because they were once socially disparaged does not mean their lives will not end up better than anyone else's. In fact, it was the upper classes that managed all of the property and employees that did not have time to arrive at their goal. They kept holding on, adding up, making profits, and expanding their egos to fill their unfathomable souls that when the real deal came by, they hardly noticed it.

Sometimes, on your way forward, you have to stop and smell the roses. See what others are doing because your assumptions are not necessarily reality. You must know what others are doing and what they have done, especially if they are very different from you. This is because what you do not know or seem to understand might soon become very clear and essential for your progress and success. This is an extremely important step towards fulfilling your life's purpose and living with a peace of mind.

Be Truthful Towards Yourself

Many people never find their purpose on earth or achieve satisfaction in life because they spend most of it lying to themselves. I do not encourage lying under any circumstance, but the worst thing anyone can do is to lie to themselves. When you lie to yourself for too long, you begin to believe and live the lie. In the process, you end up becoming what you are not or living a life that is not meant for you.

I have met a lot of people on the heavy side who claim they are that way because of genetics. Well, even if they do have fat genes in their family line, diet and exercise can still fix the problem. The actual issue is the quantity and the quality of their food and their exercise regiment, or lack there of. However, this is no secret! These large people know all this information from medical journals, weight clubs, and the media, but they still choose to believe it is their genes. By blaming it on genes, they are indirectly escaping the responsibility of taking the necessary steps of stopping or reducing their love of eating. Instead, they blame it on their ancestors through inheritance, thereby claiming that they are powerless against the condition of their circumstance.

Millions of people know exactly what they need to be doing to head towards the right direction of finding their purpose, but they keep lying to themselves about what they love too much to let go. In the process, they fail to realize that it is that very thing that they love to much that is holding them back in life. It can be pornography, sex, masturbation, prostitution, money, friends, family, alcohol, drugs, property, food, schooling, magazines, and even television. Every form of addiction is bad.

Anything done in too much excess can be bad for you and habit forming. Preventing addiction is very difficult to accomplish no matter who you are. It not only takes good discipline and determination, it also requires total control of ones destiny in the spiritual realm. Too much of one thing or anything is an addiction. An addiction is anything you are involved in that is unnecessary for your physical, mental, and spiritual growth. Whatever is contrary to your growth towards a successful and peaceful life is a hindrance that needs to be eliminated by any means necessary, even if it means starting over from the beginning and laying a better foundation.

The time and energy used to enjoy all those unnecessary substances, habits, or situations are ultimately preventing or delaying people from focusing on their purpose in life. Even when people know what they need to be doing, they end up not doing it or not maximizing their potential while doing it. This is because this unnecessary involvement eventually misleads their choices by clouding their judgment of life.

These unnecessary activities are actually the parasites of life. It is like a host plant that has a parasite attached to it. The parasite does absolutely nothing for the plant and competes against it for sunlight, nutrients, space, air, and water. As time goes on, it will either restrict the growth of the host plant or kill it completely. Unnecessary events or activities you think nobody see or are no one's business will eventually prevent you from living with a peace of mind. In the Christian world, these activities or events are called sins. They are usually not indicative of a physical problem, but a spiritual one.

Many people have tried, but were incapable of staying away from sin. So they make up all kinds of stories to justify their actions, and try to make their behavior appear culturally or socially acceptable. The reason why many can not vocalize their situation is because all they believe in is the physical world. They fail to realize that there is nothing in the physical that has not already manifested itself in the spiritual. The physical is just a transformation of the spiritual. There is nothing an individual does physically that has not yet been done in the spirit. Whatever you do physically has already been decided upon in your inner most being. Your action is just a manifestation of the decision. To change these outcomes, you need to redirect your spirit through prayers towards God in the spiritual realm. It is only through the readjustment of your spirit and aligning it with God that you can take control of your physical hindrances.

The eventual control of your physical hindrances is usually based on your transformation in attitude and belief. You will find out that results begin to change for the better when you readjust your actions and reactions to yourself, people, and situations. It usually changes for the best if your attitude and belief is aligned with God towards your life's purpose.

There was once a young and ambitious boy who felt it was time for him to become a man. Against his father's advice, he took what was rightfully his and set off to a distant land to prove himself right and worthy. He had money but did not possess wisdom and knowledge. It was not long that his wealth and inexperience attracted the wrong friends. Soon, all his money and investments were wasted, and his friends left him all alone in search for another soul to destroy. He was the son of a noble man with many properties and servants, and while he did not only loose the ability to attract people to him, he was now socially lower than his father's servants. Not only was he lonely and homeless, he began to eat the food served to pigs. This continued until one day, he decided to tell himself the bitter truth. He realized that he did not have the experience to be on his own that early in life, and he had failed in his mission. He decided to throw away the mask of pride that once clouded his reasoning and replaced it with a crown of humility.

He became so humble that he said he was going to return to his father and request that he should become a servant instead of a son. He also accepted the fact that even the servants in his father's house had better housing, food, income, and peace than he had in his current condition. It was also after he changed his attitude and belief by telling himself the truth that his life began to turn around for the better. At the end, he did not only have hope for a fresh beginning, but he was received with huge celebration as a son instead of a servant because he was eventually aligned to his life's purpose (Luke 15: 11-31).

He was not a man that was meant to cater to pigs in the filth, he was never meant to lack money, and he was not born for friends to run away from. His mother did not conceive him to be homeless or feast with swine, and neither was it his purpose to become a servant, even in his father's house. But I tell you that if he had not told himself the truth, he would have lived from one lie to the next trying to force things to become right, until he got to a point of no return while living the life of another.

Many people run into this kind of mess. They get too proud or comfortable where they are, and refuse to make the necessary changes, despite the fact that they know that they are heading towards a dead end. If the young man had refused to tell himself the truth and was trying to force a result out of hopelessness, he might have ended up rearing pigs for a living and claimed that it was his calling. He might also have taken to a life of crime to make a living or may have taken his own life if he felt he was too proud for anything else.

It is only after we have confessed the truth to ourselves that the change of attitude and belief becomes inevitable. There is a difference between knowing the truth and confessing or telling yourself the truth. You may know the truth and not accept it, but he who has confessed the truth to himself has also accepted it. Transformation only begins with acceptance and after acceptance come change. When you change, you begin to get aligned with God's purpose for your life. You begin to realize that you do not settle for the things you used to. You begin to see things that never existed in old environments and circumstances. You begin to hear voices of ideas you had never tuned to before. You who used to run after ideas and progressive results will now have those same or different ideas and progressive results running for you. One thing a truthful person will always tell you is that life is always filled with problems until you die. When you transform yourself through truth and alignment with God's purpose for your life, it does not mean that problems stop coming. It means that you have moved from a problem of lack of ideas and opportunity to a problem of abundant resources, and sometimes wonder what to do with it. When that time comes, you are no longer praying for anything, you are now praying for guidance and direction towards a specific purpose. Ultimately, you begin to go to places you never went to before, or never knew existed or could be reached. Then, people will begin to wonder why things are just favoring you and why everything seems to sit at your finger tips. This is because you are not only a person who has found his or her mission, but you are obviously accomplishing your purpose here on earth.

In the ancient times, one of the most obvious groups of people who were easily categorized as "sinners" by the population were the tax collectors. We all know that no human is perfect in their abilities, so they were never expected to collect the exact tax required and they would not collect anything less either. So their main occupation was to intentionally collect what was more than what was technically owed.

There was once a man who was a chief tax collector in the region. This meant that he not only

Living With A Peace of Mind

specialized in recruiting and hiring "sinners," he also trained them. He usually monitored their progress, and ultimately, they reported their profitable collections to him. On one occasion, this chief heard that Jesus was passing by, so he climbed on a tree so that he could take a look. As Jesus walked by, he called to the chief by name and requested to spend time at the chief's house. A lot of people were opposed to the thought of the "prince of peace" staying in a house of sin. Their opposition was justified. Sin hinders peace. Sin, or lack of purpose, must be destroyed for peace to reign. Why must a man who hinders others have peace in his house? This is a man who not only collects more than he should for himself, but ultimately, prevents others from utilizing their savings and investments adequately. Does a man who prevents others from living with a peace of mind deserve to have that same peace of mind?

Regardless, Jesus went in and stayed with the chief. It was not long afterwards that the man made a change in his life. He made it clear that he was going to give the poor, and to each person he had robbed of his savings and investments, he was going to pay back four times. What!!! An almighty chief "sinner" promoted to a philanthropist over night? Whoa!!! This must be amazing – such is the power of Christ (Luke 19: 1-10)!

The truth of the matter is that he was already a philanthropist in the spirit before Jesus even entered the picture. You see misguided souls that build wealth at the expense of others never live a life of peace. In fact, they have lied to themselves, convincing themselves that it is the proper way of life, because they have lost their actual purpose on earth and need their wealth to compensate for the emptiness within. Some of them even make it a career to oppress and prevent others from achieving their peace of mind by robbing them of the foundation of their dreams. These kinds of people do not like the truth and will never accept it because it reminds them of their deviation from their actual path. It also exposes them to their numerous worshippers that they know are also being led astray by their worldly possessions.

This kind of person would not want to see Jesus or let Jesus see him. If he knew Jesus was coming to his town or through his street, he would even leave town or isolate himself indoors. It is because the tax collector realized that all his wealth did not bring him fulfillment that he allowed himself to grasp the truth, which was that he had to give back what he had stolen. He also had to use the profits he had gained from the investments of what he had stolen to improve the life of the poor and needy. This is the mindset of many philanthropists who crave the amassing of wealth. They begin to give back when they realize that all their riches, without peace and the love of the people, is meaningless.

It was because of this truth that the collector came out of his house and climbed up on a tree to see Jesus. It was because of this same truth that he told himself that made Jesus to see him in the midst of the multitude around him. I would like to believe for every rich man that climbs a tree, there should at least be a hundred poor people or youngsters on the trees as well. But that day, there was something different about this rich man who had nothing better to do, like counting his precious gold coins, than to climb a tree publicly just to see a son of a carpenter who pays taxes walking by. He was a changed man, and I am sure that he had already confessed the truth in his spirit to himself, weeks before Jesus saw his physical manifestation on the tree. This is the very reason why one rich tax collector who made all the excuses in the world realized why he could not achieve peace of mind by attending the banquet, while another tax collector, who was also among the destitute and rejected, attended the banquet as a philanthropist.

Living With A Peace of Mind

It is never how well you started but how well you finish. We all came into this world not knowing our purpose or the direction to achieve it. We are like sheep without a Shepard just roaming the grassland in search of pasture and water with the hope of avoiding snakes, thieves, and wolves or foxes in sheep's' clothing. Many will be bitten or killed while some will just wonder out of bearing. Some will have lots of different grasses to eat, but will always worry about their safety from attacks. Some will not have to worry because they have found the Shepard that leads them to the exact grass needed for their growth and nourishment, and provides protection from all attacks. A lot of sheep do see the Shepard, but some believe they can do without him, while others feel that they do not trust him. It is the sheep that has protection and eats the right grass that matures consistently and ultimately lives with a peace of mind.

Be Tactful As You Move towards Your Goal

Just because a sheep has found a Shepard does not mean it can now become senseless and do whatever it likes. Oh yes, they might say, "we have a protector so we can now go play in a snake's pit, or better yet, mingle amongst all sheep, even if they might be foxes or wolves in disguise." It does not make them right. Many people believe that because the laws of the land favor them, they have the freedom to disregard others less favored by the law. There have been many cases where one gender lies against another about sexual and physical crimes because the law favors or protects them. Spiritual, legal, and social protection is great, but must be utilized with tact for the betterment of society at large.

Remember that we live in a society were the majority does not want to hear the truth because they do not wish to know how much better off they are than those around them. Many of these people are usually the ones who are dream killers and who do not want to see others happy. One of the ways you can fall into their schemes is if you are not tactful towards fulfilling your own purpose. It has been said that he who knows you is the one that can kill you. Many will come as friends and family trying to get information under the disguise to bettering themselves, but actually seek the information to destroy you. You have to request the spirit of discernment from the spiritual heavenly planes to guide you on how to answer their questions. You must also request that your service to mankind must not be used against you. This is what the enemy of progress thrives on when you are not being tactful with you mind, mouth, and actions.

Enemies of progress come in different forms to individuals, communities, and even nations. In terms of nations, the purpose of war and colonization is not just to impose views on others, but to ultimately tax them out of their own resources. In the process, the oppressors do not only influence the culture and citizen's thinking process, they eventually dictate the pace of economical advancement, even after they are gone. It is a case of total control through the mind, body, and soul.

This issue was what the Jews faced during the occupation of the Romans over 2000 years ago, as well as many other conquered groups in the world today. Paying of tax or tithes is an act of submission to a higher authority. It does not matter if it is God, your government, or an occupying colonizer. So the Jews paying tax to Rome was a sign of total defeat politically, economically, socially, and spiritually. At this time, Jesus was supposed to be the messiah or savior of the Jews. To the Jews, of what use is a messiah in Judea if he can not free them from the oppression of the Romans.

So one day, leaders of the Jewish establishments came nicely to request the advice of the "King of the Jews." They wanted to know if the Jews should pay taxes to the Roman. This was a very devilish question from those who would have destroyed the purpose of Jesus on earth. In fact, Christ might have been sent to his grave sooner than he expected. There was really no way out of this question at all. If Jesus had told them not to pay their taxes to Rome, the experts of law that will bear witness against him in court for the charge of treason against Rome. If Jesus had told them to pay taxes to Rome, then almost all his followers who did not understand that he was not a physical, but a spiritual, messiah would have deserted him in the middle of his mission. This is because it was unclear how the messiah, who was called "King of the Jews", advise his followers to submit themselves to the forces he was supposed to have saved them from. Not only would the coward, Simon Peter, have denied him earlier, the Romans would not have needed the services of Judas Iscariot to first hand him over to the Chief Priest before sentencing him to the cross.

So in answering, Jesus was very tactful. He did not want to lose his followers and at the same time, he refused to submit to Roman rule. In fact, Jesus fought Roman and Jewish rule through civil disobedience throughout the scriptures. He asked them to get the coin used for paying taxes and asked them to identify the inscription. According to the people, it was a Roman inscription and it was a Roman coin. Then Jesus reasoned with the people that if the coin was not a Jewish coin, why hold on to it. He insisted that it was a Roman coin and must be given back to Rome. He then asked one of the disciples to go ahead and give Rome what belonged to it for both of them. It was clear in his response and action that he gave to Rome and can not be charged for treason, but at the same time he rejected Rome's lordship over them and kept his followers. He ended up killing two birds with one stone (Matthew 22: 15-22).

Now, in ancient times, the Samaritans believed that God should be worshipped on the mountain where Moses received the Ten Commandments, but the Jews believed that God must be worshipped in the temple that Solomon built and where the ark of the Lord resided. This was the main division between the Samaritans and the Jews. It was a disparity between their religion and their system of belief. Because of this petty feud, two peoples of the same ancestry raised their children to dislike one another (John 4: 9 & 12).

Now, keep in mind that the priests were the traditional rulers of the Jewish nation, who were now basically puppets for the Roman Governor ruling Judea, while the Levites were the blood relatives of Moses and Aaron, who were a descendant of Levi (Exodus 2: 1-10, Numbers 3: 1-13). So when ever Jesus talked about priests or Levites in his parables, he was actually questioning the political and religious leaders and how they represented the Jewish nation during the Roman occupation and oppression.

There was once an occasion where a man needed advice from Jesus. He wanted to know who his neighbor was. You would have thought that he was an uneducated fool. To the surprise of many, he was another expert of the law. "My God!!! Some might have said, "Which law school did he go to? I can not believe that during law school, he never came across the word "neighbor". I hope he knows what defendant means?"

At this time, many Jewish people were beginning to get weary of Jesus. They felt that if he was the messiah, he should raise up against the Romans instead of scoring minute defiant points against the Jewish establishment. They were also tried of him changing their customs by putting value in the lives of their low elements in society such as prostitutes, lepers, Gentiles, and handicaps. So when they came to ask him about who their neighbor was, they were hoping he would name some of the groups considered inferior or unclean by Jewish standards so that they could accuse him of being a rebel and a deviant.

Jesus understood where this "scholar of the law" was going, so he told him a story of a Jewish man who was beaten up by robbers in his own land. While he laid down dying, a priest and a Levite came by at separate times, and when they saw the dying man, they quickly passed him, by taking the other side of the road. It was not long that a Samaritan came by and he picked the man up. The Samaritan did not only take the Jewish man to get medical attention, he also paid for it. He then asked the man with the legal title who his neighbor was in the story, and he agreed that it was the Samaritan. So it was not Jesus who told the Jewish crowd that the Samaritan was their neighbor, it was their legal expert who said so. So, not only could they not accuse Jesus of anything, but I doubt if anyone would take the lawyer to court. So the attempt to disturb Jesus and his purpose was stopped dead in its tracks (Luke 10: 25-37).

We should be very tactful in dealing with our adversaries or those who want to hinder us from fulfilling our purpose here on earth. We must also realize that when we reject anyone based on any form of difference, we are also a hindrance to ourselves. The Jews put too much emphasis on their priests and temples, and on Moses and the law, but yet discriminated against their own blood (Jesus and his Disciples) and the Gentiles. In the story, it was not their glorious priests, teachers, or the family of Moses that came to their aid to preserve them for their purpose; it was the Samaritan that made sure the Jew remained alive to fulfill his purpose. Tact and open mindedness is a must when living with a peace of mind.

You Must Add Value to Your Life

One of the diseases that plague a lot of people is complacency. It is one thing to know and find your purpose, but it is another to follow through. While you follow through and head towards your goal, you need to add value to your life and the lives around you. It other words, you need to take responsibility for enriching other people's lives as you go along. A man that can not give hope and peace to those who see and touch him, irrespective of how much money he has, has not yet found his purpose. It is your responsibility, as you head towards your destiny, to broaden your network and knowledge on how to better serve those around you.

Goodness, godliness, and success are interwoven and can never be separated. The purpose for successful people, who have found their purpose and are living with a peace of mind, is to lay the foundation for many others to succeed in finding their purpose. This can only be achieved when the people who have found their purpose have broadened their own knowledge and experience to the extent that all who hear and see them can be blessed by words and deed.
On your way to living a fulfilled life, which is like the trunk of a tree, you must grow a lot of branches. A trunk takes water and nutrients from the roots to the branches to keep the leaves alive. In return, the leaves bring the circulation of air throughout the entire plant. A tree that does not breathe is dead. Ultimately, the trunk of the tree must first serve the leaves before its can be classified as a living tree. It is not just enough for the trunk to grow upward towards the sun and to be huge and strong; it must also grow branches to serve the leaves that also take in sunlight and produce food. Otherwise, its life will not be successful because it will not live very long, if it ever lives at all. Knowledge is not just the highest form of wealth; it is the branch that gives hope to many leaves in their quest for success in finding their purpose towards living with a peace of mind.

Living With A Peace of Mind

A man who keeps his knowledge and experience to himself is dead. He is not only a waste, but a hindrance to all those whom he comes in contact with. He is the salt that has lost its saltiness, a light that is dim, and a trunk that has refused to grow branches. You are not living in peace until you have touched the lives of those around you. Your life is not fulfilled or purposeful until many are being blessed by your activities. A man that has found his purpose must become multi-lateral. He goes and acquires for others. He is not a slave or a fool either. In the process of gathering information needed to better himself and his purpose, he educates, informs, and assists others, who require the knowledge, in their quest towards their purpose.

Many of the disciples of Jesus were not very educated and influential men when they were recruited into His purpose. There was no evidence that they could read or write, and they were obviously not very good speakers, at least publicly. It was after they were filled with the Holy Spirit that they became men of purpose, courage, and direction. Many of them, like a lot of us, hinder ourselves with fear because we have no knowledge about how the system works. We do not possess the necessary skills and technique to maneuver our way through circumstances. So many of us give up or become career followers, instead of accomplished leaders. Despite the fact that the disciples were filled with the Holy Spirit, they still lacked the skills and expertise to preach the gospel to the end of the earth as Jesus commissioned them to do. They had their importance in the spread of Christianity, but I must testify that it was not very effective, as least for a while. As time went on, with the help of the Spirit and experience, you could see the maturity in disciples, such as Peter and James (Acts 1:8, Galatians 2:11-14).

There was a man named Saul, whose name was later changed to Paul. As far as I am concerned, he was the greatest apostle of all. He wrote more books than any other writer in the bible and in fact, he is basically the writer of the New Testament. He did not only help establish churches in many Jewish and Gentile cities, but also wrote them numerous letters of encouragement in the New Testament to stay strong in the infant faith against strong Jewish and Roman oppositions. But why would a man who was not even one of the twelve chosen by Jesus became the most influential apostle in taking the word of God to the ends of the earth? This is a man who never lived with or walked with Jesus. How did this come to be? What kind of value did he possess in his life to be recruited by Jesus himself after Christ's departure into heaven?

While the chosen apostles were being groomed for their purpose, Paul was already rooted and equipped for his purpose, but he was in a wrong profession to achieve it. During the time of Paul, the ancient Roman Empire was a mighty power, and they controlled most of the known world of the time.

Under Roman rule, education and citizenship were of extreme importance, just like any other civilized nation of today. So who ever controlled the Roman mindset, culture, government, or religion controlled or influenced a lot of people, and, therefore, was quite powerful.

My Grandmother's friend always told people that it was the rat inside the house that always showed those outside how to get in. For the word of God to reach the ends of the earth from a Roman colony of Judea, it first had to take root and survive in the Roman environment. For the word of God to get anywhere from Jerusalem as a product of Jerusalem, it had to survive there as well. It could have been transported to a different location outside the Roman Empire, but then, it would no longer be tied to Jerusalem, and

Living With A Peace of Mind

Jerusalem would have lost its flavor (from a Christian perspective). Jesus' commission to the apostles was to start from Jerusalem and spread to the ends of the earth, so the word of God had no choice but to survive in Jerusalem.

To accomplish this, Jesus recruited someone who had the ability to physically transform what has already being manifested in the spiritual realm. It was going to be someone who could hardly be opposed by the Romans and their system. Unlike the twelve apostles, Paul was a Roman citizen, he was extremely well educated, he had dedicated himself to God, he knew his purpose on earth, and he was prepared to die for his purpose before Jesus visited him. He represented the other side of how God works. Sometimes God takes people through what they need to know and leads them to their purpose, while others go all out to acquire what they believe they need in the wrong places until God brings them to their purpose. Paul was an example of the later.

Paul was educated as a Pharisee and was a son of a Pharisee. He was taught the strict rules, laws, and customs of the Jewish faith. He was a reader and writer of both Hebrew and Roman. The Pharisee and Priests worked together with the Roman officials in governing Judea, so written communication and translation were of utmost importance for all members of the party. I would not be surprised if it was not a stage one requirement by the Roman system for all ethic leaders to be able to speak and write in Roman. As a Roman citizen, it meant that Paul could travel anywhere without a pass or other restrictions. It also meant he could not be arrested for whatever he said, wrote, or did – except when he spoke against Rome itself. All Roman citizens were also exempted from flogging unless they were found guilty. This was usually used as a tool of intimidation. Unlike the apostles, this meant that Paul had total freedom of speech to carry out his purpose without the slightest opposition from the governing Roman Empire (Acts 22:22-29, Acts 23: 6, Acts 26: 4-5, Philippians 3: 4-6).

Paul had already known his purpose and that was to set himself apart for God. His life was dedicated not just to the temple of God, but also to the laws of his people. He was ready to defend God, the laws of Moses, and the Jewish way even if it means killing Christians. To Paul, and many of the Jews of the time, Christianity was a large thorn in the Jewish side. It was an insult to take a Jewish commoner, who died on the cross like a criminal, to be the son of God and the savior of the Jewish people. Jesus was considered a liar who promised freedom but died in the hands of the oppressors of his people. Some thought that anyone who followed such a God must be sub-human and did not deserve to live. It was enough dealing with the ever-constant Roman oppression, but to have some rebellious Jews following teachings of a dead lunatic was too much. Paul's purpose on earth was to fight the fight of righteousness against anything trying to lure God's people away from God (Acts 8: 1-2, Acts 9: 1-2).

Paul already had the qualities the apostles needed to carry out the great commission for Christ, but he was on the wrong side of the fence. All Jesus had to do was to show him that He was the very God he was fighting for and that He was the reason why Paul had a purpose in life to begin with. The very things Paul had sworn to defend with his life, the Laws of Moses, Judaism, Israel, God's covenant with Abraham, and the words of the Prophets, are actually meaningless without Jesus. The purpose of their existence was to direct Jesus' coming. It was after Paul realized this that he became a fulfilled man. He altered the course of human history. He became a man completely living with a peace of mind for the rest of his days. He converted more people, wrote more letters, visited more places, and affected more lives than the twelve apostles put together. It was because of

Paul, a man that once killed Christians, the Roman religion changed to Christianity and is why Christianity eventually became the world's largest religion.

When a person has added value in his or her life, his or her purpose will come looking for the individual. Your responsibility as a human being is to add value to your life that others can utilize to find their purpose towards serving and improving their communities. It does not matter if you have found your purpose or not, but you must intentionally add value in your life. If you have found your purpose, increase your values and worth for others. If you have not found your purpose, still increase your value and worth for others to utilize, and like Paul, your purpose will come looking for you. This is a simple spiritual formula in the supernatural realm that is above all human understanding and must manifest itself in the physical over time.

A lot of people have thought of suicide or fallen into alcoholism and drugs when their degrees and investments are not yielding what they had expected them to. They fall into all types of despair and begin to become harmful to everyone by intentionally doing things that they know would hurt, not only themselves, but everyone else around them. Their intention is to punish themselves for failing to excel and those around them for not coming to their aid in their time of need. Some go as far as taking their own lives without imagining the effect it will have on their loved ones who failed to be of any constructive assistance.

The secret to defeating failure and suicide is to be transparent and flexible in adding value to your life. If your degree or your trade is not achieving the success and fulfillment you expect it to, you need to network and diversify. So many people are not even using their degree to make a living. Many people going to college and choosing their degrees have not even finished defining themselves yet. Some of them, who have an iota of an idea about what they were called to do on earth, are still too immature or young to withstand the conforming hurricanes of societal pressures. These can be peer pressures, parental expectations, or societal definitions of success.

If this is you, when your degree and trade fails, simply redefine yourself in your current age and circumstance then make a move. Before you make that move, I recommend that you consult the spiritual realm to align your move with God's destiny for your life, or I guarantee that move will be a second waste of time and energy. If one door is locked try another, until the spirit of God shows you the correct door to open. The funny thing is that the door is usually an old familiar opening that has always been there, but you were so used to it you never felt the need to open it at all. The right door, over time, may have became too familiar, old, or dull, and was not as attractive as the modern doors you walked passed as you journeyed through the corridors of life.

It does not matter if you go through ten doors to find the door that leads you to your purpose in life; those ten doors are unconsciously adding value to your life. Even if you do not use all the knowledge and skills you have gathered over time, you will always have an opportunity to bless others with those precious experiences as they move on towards their own purpose.

In very early times, it was not popular to have a first name and a last name. People were usually named in reference to their father, like James, son of Zebedee, or in reference to their occupation, like John the Baptist or the Baptizer, or in reference to their city, like Jesus of Nazareth or Joseph of Arimathea. It was the Romans that began the culture of using first and last names, which we still use today, for easy taxation and identification. This is because there could be many Zebedees who have sons named James, or several Johns that love the act of baptizing, or multiple Josephs in Arimathea. So the problem for the Romans became how to differentiate every individual in order not to lose out on taxes. So it became, for example, James Zebedee, the fisherman, who lives in Galilee.

The Roman officials, their citizens, and their ethnic officials in their colonies had to follow this naming system during the times of Jesus. It was an easy way to recognize who was "Romanized" or who were their citizens, since many of the non-Romans had not yet conformed to this system. Julius Caesar and Pontius Pilate are very good examples. Assuming all the original disciples were Jewish, which I believe the all were, why is it that only Judas had a first name and a last name, thereby following the Roman system. He was called Judas Iscariot, while the other disciples either had just their first name by itself, or it was attached to their occupation or to their father. As you read further, you will notice in the scriptures that Judas Iscariot was the treasurer for the ministry of Jesus and the entire group (John 13:29, Luke 6: 13-16).

In Judea, it was very uncommon to see a Jewish commoner in the gathering of the elite, except when they were servants of a noble man or were invited in by a noble man for whatever reason. Either way, the commoner was not free to do or say much because he was under the responsibility of the noble that invited him or whom he attended with. Earlier in Jesus' ministry, before his name was widely known, when they were in the gathering of the Pharisees, Sadducees, and Scribes, there is no mention of Jesus being invited to any special events. This is why people always asked his disciples what Jesus was doing among tax collectors and sinners.

The most educated and proficient disciple must have been familiar with both the Roman and Jewish ways of doing things. The only two disciples that had the clout to measure up to the Pharisees and tax collectors were Matthew and Judas Iscariot. Matthew would be likely because he was a tax collector and Judas Iscariot because the documentation of his name in history and the Bible speak for itself. We must also remember that on the last supper, it was Judas Iscariot that was eating from the same dish as Jesus. Was this the usual position at dinner time or it was a memorable time together before their separation? Either way, it testifies to the value and importance of Judas to the ministry and purpose of Jesus on earth.

In whatever you achieve here on earth, you must always add value to you life to arrive at your purpose. It does not matter if it ends up positive or if it is interpreted as negative. From a Christian perspective, what sets Jesus apart from all other deities, Prophets, and holy men, apart from his virgin birth, is his crucifixion for humanity and his resurrection. Just as the purpose of John was to introduce a new order of worship of God through Christ, and just after accomplishing his purpose he died, the purpose of Judas Iscariot was to guarantee the crucifixion of Christ. Judas Iscariot is the most misunderstood, the most underappreciated, but yet, the most important of the twelve disciples to the ministry of Jesus on earth. We must remember that Christ told the disciples that those who serve are the greatest (Luke 22: 24-27).

Jesus came to die for humanity and reconcile it back to God. This was his only purpose on earth, which he discovered and lived for in his last three years. The truth of the matter is that Jesus had to die at the hands of the Jewish establishment because he was obviously a threat to their way of life. The problem was how they were going to kill him. They could not arrest Jesus during the day because the people who were related to those whom he had healed and improved their lives would revolt. They could not catch him at night because Jesus did not stay in one place. Someone had to hand him over if he was going to fulfill his purpose for humanity on the cross. Who among Jesus' comrades was qualified for such a job? Who among them was intelligent enough to understand what had to be done and had the credential and credibility to get the attention of the high priest and elders? Was it Peter, who could not even tell a servant girl on the street that he was with Jesus? Could it be James or John, who both fell asleep, along with Peter, just before Jesus' capture in Gethsemane, instead of staying awake to pray? Why not Bartholomew, whose name appears about once in each of the gospel without saying a word or doing a thing (Mark 14: 66-72, Matthew 26: 36-46)?

    The only man among the twelve who had enough value to his life that could fulfill this purpose was Judas Iscariot. The only one of the twelve, who was documented in history with the credentials of the Romans of the time, was Judas Iscariot. He was a man whom I suspect was educated by Roman standards, was a writer and reader of Hebrew, Aramaic, and Roman, and performed some task for Rome. I would believe that this task was tax collecting, which most ethnic people of that caliber did at the time, and that must be why Jesus made him the treasurer of the group. The combination of all these values, being trusted by Jesus to keep the group's money, and sharing Jesus' dish at the last supper, reveals to me the importance of Judas Iscariot to the ministry and mission of Jesus. Why didn't the other disciples prevent Judas from leaving the last supper to go betray Jesus after Jesus told him to go on with it? Could it be that they understood his mission and purpose to Jesus' cause? Could it be that they really though that Jesus was sending him on an errand, or they were they so far beneath him in social status they dared not oppose him (John 13: 18-30, Mark 14: 17-21)?

Many scholars have argued that the act of Judas Iscariot was an agreement between Jesus and him. Others have claimed that Judas wanted to give Jesus an audience to face the Jewish leaders to proclaim his Kingdom and new ways of doing things, but most of the modern Christians consider Judas a traitor. Which ever group you belong to, it is clear that he handed Jesus to the high priest. It was his purpose to fulfill, and that is the ultimate reason why the son of God chose him and put him in a position to do it. The lesson here is that

Living With A Peace of Mind

whatever you were put here to fulfill, will never be accomplished until you have aligned your life with God and your purpose is revealed to you. In the process of doing this, you must add and build value to your life in order to have the credential to carry out the task that needs to be accomplished. No task is easy, even when it is a journey of living with a peace of mind.

Utilize Every Opportunity

For Accomplishment

It is not always your degree, the job you want, or your ancestral family trade that might lead you to a fulfilled life. You have to be prepared and available to open as many doors as possible. This would add value to your life as you discover your God given purpose to impact and influence the lives of those around and about you. Even if you stumble on your destiny and you are enjoying the fruits of it, you still need that spiritual guidance and assurance. This is because you need to know if it is what you should focus your time and energy on in order to avoid all forms of distractions and deviations that might lead to sorrow and regret. There is no place too small or too low to build value to your life. I am not trying to look down on any individual or encourage anybody to be less than what God's purpose is for his or her life. The point I am making is that be whatever you need to be morally to make it through today as you align yourself with God to climb up towards that purpose that will separate you from the rest of humanity. In every situation and condition, be it good or bad, rich or poor, happy or sad, progress or regression, as long as you are genuinely doing your best, you must give glory to God. This is because everything is temporary as life grows and changes, but ultimately, the end result is to bring glory to God and peace of mind and joy to all those who are living their purpose through their alignment with God.

There was once a boy named David. He was not only the least among his brothers; it was his responsibility as the least to walk the family's herd of sheep in the desert. His job was to walk the dumb sheep to get grass and water, and at the same time protect them from carnivores and snakes. All this he did in a desert region. In fact, when a prophet came from God to anoint him for Kingship, his very own father called out every son he could imagine, but left David in isolation with sheep in the desert. Wouldn't unemployment be better than David's situation? He was stuck out in the hot sun, where it was almost impossible to grow anything, with smelly sheep for companions.

He was forced to look for greens and water in a wasteland to sustain the family business and his father still didn't think well of him. He belonged to a Shepard family and it was his activities that brought food to the table and paid the bills. Yet, when honor came for him, he was relegated to the background by his own father. Not even one of his brothers remembered the youngster that slaved day and night in the midst of bears and lions to make sure that their family's head was not covered in shame economically (1 Samuel 17: 28 & 34).

In one of the battles where the Philistines came to oppress the Israelites, David's father sent him to take food to his brothers at the war front. When he got there, he saw a giant insulting God. This offended David and he asked his older brother about it. The older brother took pleasure in reminding him that he was Shepard boy and not a soldier, and he had no business at war fronts but in the desert hill tending to sheep. He then turned and asked the other soldiers about the giant.

After he was informed about the giant's disrespect to God and his nation, he decided to take on the giant himself. The soldier gave him a sword and an armor to put on, but it was too heavy for him, so he decided to use what he knew best, which was the sling. He went to battle against the giant by first aligning himself to God. With the word of God on his lips and a sling in his hand, he killed the giant. From that day on he became the nation's favorite person, over even the King of the nation and the General of the Army. It was based on this accomplishment that he was catapulted from a desert sheep herder to his purpose in life of becoming the second, and greatest, king of Israel (1 Samuel 17).

We should never worry about where we are in life. We can cry and be sad a little, just to water the eyes and give it something to do. Ultimately, we must get up and look for something else to accomplish, no matter how trivial. This is to boost up our self-esteem and confidence. It was his experience of tending to senseless sheep in the desert that gave him the knowledge of dealing with people that have the capacity to reason when he got to the throne. It was his loneliness in the desert that gave him the courage to withstand rejection from his family. It is the barren environment in the wasteland that gave him the perseverance to survive in times of adversary. It was his experience in using a sling to kill and drive off lions and bears that gave him the confidence to face the giant. After all, what is the courage or strength of a man compared to a beast such as a lion or a bear? The very things you cry and curse

God about in your lowly places are the foundations of your greatness in finding your purpose and following it through.

When you are determined to live with a peace of mind by finding your purpose and utilizing the value of your earned skills to serve mankind, even a slave will become a president in a foreign land, and a maid will become a chief executive officer of a global firm. All you have to do is to choose goodness and godliness, align yourself with God, and be prepared and determined to serve your fellowman with all that you possess from within so that God might be glorified.

There are a lot of giants in our lives that prevent us from getting to our destinies or even finding our God-given purpose on earth. But the truth of the matter is that these giants in our lives are the minuscule issues that we are so familiar with in our comfort zones.

The two main giants in many of our lives are family and culture. This was true for David also, as his story shows. Everyone would expect that the family is a place of refuge, respect, and encouragement, but from experience and talking to a lot of people, the family sometimes tends to be more of a problem than solution. David's family did not only put him down or not think much of him; they almost robbed him of his opportunity to open the door of his destiny. They did not only remind him that he was a Shepard boy or ignore him on the day he was to be blessed; his senior brother unconsciously tried to prevent him from killing the giant, which is obviously what he was born to do.

Culture, heritage, and traditions can become a very dangerous and hideous crime. Care must be taken to modify them with the present needs of an era to act as a better foundation towards a brighter future. People sometimes want to do things the way it is usually done or the way their father's always did it. This is not very wise because it can either eliminate our competitive advantage as a whole, or slip us into warring fractions. We must always evaluate and re-evaluate ourselves periodically in order to be the best that we can be to God, ourselves, and our community. Relying too much on culture, tradition, and heritage without planning for the future will not only weaken the group but might build resentments from within.

It was the culture of the time to wear armor and carry swords when soldiers went to war.

Living With A Peace of Mind

Armor may include a helmet, breast plate, shin guard, shield, spear, sword, and matching shoes. It was tradition to wear this armor in battle for protection from injury and death. It was heritage to keep armor for pride and souvenirs, or pass it on to your descendants. If David had followed traditions that day, he would have become a dead piece of meat instead of becoming the king of his people. The armor was just too heavy for him when he tried it on. I am sure he could not even walk straight and move his body freely. How would he have survived in this against a giant on the giant's own terms? Sometimes you have to be honest with yourself and be the person that you are, using your experiences from the past and your known skills to advance towards your destiny. David went like the Shepard boy that he was, and used the sling that he always used to chase away and kill wild beasts that were five time stronger than any giant.

    The Israelites did not have chariots like the Egyptians, Babylonians, or the Philistines. It was always their military culture to strategically hide in the hills until they could attack their opponents when they least expected a strike. This is why David has referred sometimes in scripture to the hill as a refuge, which sometimes failed him. This was also the technique the Israelites were using against the Philistines. Since the chariots are meant for open field warfare and not the hills, the giant thought by abusing them and their God, they would come out and fight. But it did not work because it was not the culture of the Jews to attack when they had no competitive advantage. When your enemy understands your culture which you are so proud of, and knows the way you think and react, you have basically lost your competitive advantage. This might mean a change or modification in your culture is required to arrive at your purpose. It was God who sent a Shepard and not a soldier. It was God who used the unexpected sling and not the comfortable sword and shield. It was also God who used a desert boy, not the mighty men of honor to uproot the Philistines that day.

The many problems we think we have in our lives are not our problems at all. They are actually our accomplishments. We only fail to see them as what they really are because by nature, we are negative and like to believe we have problems where there are really none. The giant in David's story was not a problem at all; he was David's accomplishment to catapult him to becoming king. Our problems are usually our family, friends, culture, peer pressure, and societal expectations, not the mountains we are meant to climb to put us on top of the world. We are not expected to cry about racism, sexism, tribalism, corruption, mismanagement of national resources, police brutality, drugs, bad government, or even wrongful purpose for war. We are supposed to rise above all these issues and conquer them all. A nation with citizens that are oppressors and where some are oppressed is a nation that is not aligned with God's will. It is also a nation that had fractions, and a nation that might ultimately fail in accomplishing its divine purpose.

      Like with David, the problems of every nation are its allies, their non-modified culture and heritage, and their failure to include God in whatever they do. Your allies are like your friends and family. If you do not move with divine judgment to fulfill your destiny and have a nation living with peace of mind, you will find yourself making decisions based on the standards and expectations of your so called allies. When you do not modify your culture and heritage to be fair and just to the changes taking place within, a nation might become too fractioned in the heart to withstand any external force that may strike. Just like the Roman Empire fell at their weakest time to invading Barbarians in history, we must make economic, social, political, and educational laws that favor all citizens and guests that we have within us. It is this fairness and justice to all within our borders that brings true peace and freedom to our nation. It is the genuine solidarity of any nation that frees it from of adversaries that do not wish it well, and not pre-emptive strikes against suspected enemies.

We must go out of our way to put God in everything we do. This means if we believe in the "big-bang" theory, creationism, evolution, or atheism, we must recognize the force, nature, and spirit that put all these things in order. We must control the spiritual realm to have the result we want in the physical. We must align the nation with the spiritual realm so that God can reveal to us the steps we need to take as we achieve our purpose. If your ultimate purpose is to live at peace and be fulfilled in whatever you do physically on earth, then we must encourage every citizen to have God in their lips, minds, and actions.

About the Author

Ehimwenma E. Aimiuwu is currently an usher and a member of the Men's fellowship at the Redeemed Christian Church of God (RCCG) – Victory International Center. He is married with two children and God has revealed to him that his purpose on earth is to write books and speak at churches and schools. His aim is to uplift people and to encourage them in finding and fulfilling their destiny and purpose on earth.

His education includes a Bachelors of Arts in Anthropology and a Masters in Business Administration with a concentration in Management Information Systems from Kent State University in Ohio.

Mr. Aimiuwu has worked as a manager for various companies in corporate America. He has also taught in grade schools and colleges in the state of Georgia, USA. He is the proud author of two previous books, which are "The Political and Spiritual Purpose of the Holy Land" and "A Calabash Never Sinks". He has also had the pleasure of appearing on the African Treasures TV program on the Atlanta Interfaith Broadcast Channel, WRFG (89.3 FM) – Radio Free Georgia, and some magazines in the Atlanta Area.